# NORTH CAROLINA

GALLERY BOOKS
An Imprint of W. H. Smith Publishers Inc.
112 Madison Avenue
New York City 10016

This edition first published in U.S.
in 1991 by Gallery Books,
an imprint of W.H. Smith Publishers, Inc.
112 Madison Avenue, New York, New York 10016

053835          ISBN 0-8317-0261-3

Printed and bound in Spain

For rights information about the photographs in
this book please contact:

The Image Bank
111 Fifth Avenue, New York, NY 10003

Producer: Solomon M. Skolnick
Writer: Nancy Millichap Davies
Design Concept: Lesley Ehlers
Designer: Ann-Louise Lipman
Editor: Joan E. Ratajack
Production: Valerie Zars
Photo Researcher: Edward Douglas
Assistant Photo Researcher: Robert V. Hale
Editorial Assistant: Carol Raguso

*Title page:* An autumnal glow blankets
the Blue Ridge Mountains in this view
toward the Catawba River from Hump-
back Mountain. *Opposite:* A noteworthy
example of a Georgian Colonial public
building, the Chowan County Courthouse
in Edenton (1767) is the oldest courthouse in the state in continuous use.

Edenton's Cupola House, from which a lookout watched for approaching ships, dates from the colonial era. *Below:* This Revolutionary War cannon, like two others mounted on Edenton's sea wall, was bought from France by town patriots for the Continental Army in 177

Wherever travelers roam in North Carolina, they're seldom more than a few moment's drive from the point where thick settlement ends and the beach, farmland, or forest begins. In this rural state, more than half the residents still live outside of the towns and cities. North Carolinians, who bear the nickname "Tar Heels" for no reason on which anyone can agree, savor down-home pleasures—back porches, family reunions, barbecues. But each region is distinct in this complex state, with its two-part name, three-section geography, and four-century recorded history. The sections that make up North Carolina vary geographically: In the east the horizon stretches along the coastal plain; the Piedmont band of hills rolls across midstate; and the heights of the Blue Ridge to the west rise to the 6,684-foot summit of Mt. Mitchell, the highest point in the eastern U.S.

The coast came first, naturally, in terms of European settlement. The Outer Banks, a chain of long and narrow barrier islands, lie between the mainland and the open Atlantic along most of North Carolina's coast. Sounds and marshes separate them from the mainland. Until recently, the banks remained a remote area, so cut off that local people retained the regional English accents of their pre-Revolutionary forebears.

*Top to bottom:* St. Thomas Episcopal Church in Bath is North Carolina's oldest surviving church. The facade of St. Thomas illustrates frontier plainness at its most severe. Brick floors and gleaming wood lend the interior a classic charm.

Tryon Palace in New Bern boasts formal plantings in its garden. *Below:* A 1791 fire largely destroyed Tryon Palace, the colonial-era home of the Royal Governor which also served as the state's first capitol building, but historians and architects working from the original plans completed a meticulous reconstruction in 1959. *Opposite:* At 163 feet, Bodie Island Lighthouse stands tall on the Outer Banks.

The beautiful Elizabethan Gardens at Manteo on the Outer Banks were planted to pay tribute to the lost settlers of Roanoke including Virginia Dare, the first English child born in the American colonies. *Below:* A walkway of pre-Revolutionary brick sets off colorful flower beds in the gardens. *Opposite:* The *Elizabeth II* (above), a replica of the type of ship used to bring English colonists to Roanoke Island, lies at anchor in Manteo. An outdoor drama (below) performed beneath the summer stars since 1937, *The Lost Colony* recreates the settlement's founding—and its mysterious disappearance.

Vintage automobiles make a striking bas-relief at the Rear View Mirror Car Museum in Nags Head. *Below:* Vehicles from the mid-1900's are frozen in cast concrete on a wall at the car museum.

Today, status as a national seashore protects much of the Outer Banks from overdevelopment. The parklands and villages here attract sport fishers as well as other travelers who love the openness of the landscape, with its shifting dunes and long, bright horizons of ocean and sky.

Throughout their recorded history, the Banks have been the site of landmark events. The first English settlers in what is now the U.S. established a colony on Roanoke Island. Three groups arrived between 1585 and 1587, under the sponsorship of Sir Walter Raleigh. The first child of English parents born on American soil, Virginia Dare, made her appearance here. Then war in England delayed the supply ships, and when they finally arrived in 1590, the colonists were gone without a trace. Their end remains unknown, though theories and legends over the years have suggested every possibility from extermination to intermarriage with the region's native Americans. Their story is the plot of *The Lost Colony,* a drama enacted nightly throughout the summer at the site of Fort Raleigh, their settlement. In the nearby village of Manteo, named for a native American chieftain who befriended the settlers and even returned to England on one of the voyages, visitors can board the Elizabeth II, a replica of a sixteenth-century sailing ship like the ones

*Above:* This monument to the Wright brothers stands before Kill Devil Hill, from which they made humanity's first-ever flight. *Left:* At the Wright Brothers Memorial, a plaque sums up the brothers' pioneering achievement. *Opposite:* The Wright Brothers Memorial, a granite tower, reaches 60 feet into the Kitty Hawk sky.

WILBUR
WRIGHT
ORVILLE
WRIGHT

IN COMMEMORATION OF THE CONQUEST OF THE AIR BY

Wind-graven ridges grace the Great Dune of Cape Hatteras, the largest sand dune in the East. *Below:* Cape Hatteras Lighthouse (1870), at 208 feet the tallest in North America, overlooks treacherous Diamond Shoals. Its beam is visible 20 miles out to sea.

that sailed so hopefully to Roanoke Island.

Early in the 1700's, the Banks were among the watery hideouts of English pirates like Edward Teach, nicknamed Blackbeard, who troubled the coast with his raids. Blackbeard died off Okracoke Island in combat with Lieutenant Robert Maynard of the Royal Navy, who had been sent by the Governor of Virginia to apprehend him.

In 1903, the brothers Orville and Wilbur Wright made Kill Devil Hills, dunes near the town of Kitty Hawk, the site of the first airplane flight. A 60-foot granite monument marks the spot today. Nearby, a National Park Service museum offers glimpses of fragile gliders like the one which made that first 12-second, 120-foot flight and sheds like those in which the Wrights, bicycle-makers from Ohio, lived and worked during their seasons on the Banks.

Inland, the shady, wet reaches of the Great Dismal Swamp straddle the Virginia-North Carolina border. The densely forested wetlands, where the roots of bald cypress trees rise like knees above dark waters, actually make up not a swamp but North America's only live peat bog. Dozens of bird species, as well as a variety of reptiles including alligators and water moccasins, are protected

*Top to bottom:* The U.S.S. *North Carolina,* a World War II dreadnought, is permanently moored on the Cape Fear River. Wilmington's Zebulon Latimer House, an 1852 mansion in the Italianate style, is now the headquarters of the local historical society. In the gardens adjoining the Burgwin-Wright House (1770), paths and hedges create a patterned formality.

A onetime rice plantation south of Wilmington, Orton Plantation now boasts colorful gardens rather than flooded fields. *Below:* Fort Macon (1828–35) near Beaufort was the last Confederate stronghold on the North Carolina coast to fall to Union forces during the Civil War.

Fountains enliven the PGA/World Golf Hall of Fame in Pinehurst.

within the Dismal Swamp
National Wildlife Refuge. Nature
lovers bent on catching sight of
the region's wildlife will succeed
best in small boats on the Dismal
Swamp Canal. Dug in 1790, it is
the oldest canal still in service in
the country. Legends, which
grow best in the dark, thrive in
the Great Dismal Swamp. Des-
perate fugitives, moonshiners,
and native Americans are among
the ghosts said to haunt the
area, which was in fact a onetime favorite refuge of runaway
slaves.

Because it was settled first,
North Carolina's coast has the
state's greatest concentration of
pre-Revolutionary architecture.
The stylish eighteenth-century
houses and commercial buildings
near the waterfront in Wilmington, one of North Carolina's early
coastal ports, recall the era when
Wilmington's naval products—
tar, pitch, turpentine—were
shipped to ports worldwide. The
last Confederate harbor to be
shut down during the Civil War,
the city remains the state's most
important deep-water port. Visitors can admire the waterfront
restorations while on a riverboat
cruise. But the most intriguing
sight in town for the nautically
minded is likely to be the *U.S.S.
North Carolina*, a 728-foot dreadnought which participated in
every major naval battle in the
Pacific during World War II and
is now moored across the Cape
Fear River from Wilmington's
booming downtown.

*Above:* Built at the turn of the century,
the Pinehurst Hotel and Country Club
quickly became a mecca for golfers.
*Right:* A water hazard nestles between
the greens at one of 31 golf courses in
Pinehurst's environs.

Upriver, in the higher reaches of the coastal plain, lie better croplands than the marshy Tidewater can offer. Until the end of the Civil War, this was planters' country, covered from the early 1700's by plantations that produced rice, indigo for dye, and cotton for the English mills. Orton and Poplar Grove showcase the lush gardens and graceful interiors that typify that era. Still, there were fewer plantations in North Carolina than in the adjacent states of Virginia and South Carolina, where aristocratic traditions hold greater sway than in the Tar Heel State. In the long Southern tradition of humor by insult, North Carolinians tease their northern and southern neighbors by defining their state as "a vale of humility between two mountains of conceit."

However, New Bern, located near the coast at the head of the Neuse River, demonstrates that eighteenth-century North Carolina lifestyles could be elegant indeed. The proof is Tryon Palace, built by the Royal Governor of that name as a combined residence and administration center. This showplace of Britain's American colonies was also the site of North Carolina's first provincial congress and its first constitutional assembly. Two-thirds of the building was destroyed by a fire before 1800. The

*Above:* The James K. Polk Memorial is a reconstruction of the log house near Charlotte that was the birthplace, in 1795, of the 11th president. *Left:* The Hezekiah Alexander Homesite (1774) is the oldest surviving dwelling in the Charlotte area. *Opposite:* Charlotte's First Union Tower is among the many corporate headquarters in the Carolinas' premier financial center.

Wachovia Center

*Preceding page:* Wachovia Center, one of the Queen City's bold new high rises, soars dramatically from Charlotte's downtown. *This page, right:* A renovated church houses Charlotte's Afro-American Cultural Center. Its program highlights the contributions of black North Carolinians to the region. *Below:* The steeple of the First Presbyterian Church (1894) soars above surrounding trees.

original plans turned up in New York in 1939, and now, an ambitious and imaginative reconstruction of the missing parts recreates the spirit of Tryon Palace in the days before Josiah Martin, the last Royal Governor, fled it for the safety of a British warship at the beginning of the Revolution. New Bern's historic brick houses and churches preserve the flavor of the era when clipper ships left its wharves bound for Salem and Boston.

The Piedmont was settled later than the coast and, for the most part, not by planters. This hilly midstate region has traditionally been the heart of the state's small-farm way of life. Its position at the fall line of the rivers that flow toward the coastal plain—the Tar, the Neuse, the Trent, and the forbiddingly named Cape Fear—gave Piedmont folk access to the water power that made possible the industrial expansion of the nineteenth century. After the Civil War, the state's output of cotton began to find its way to North Carolina mills for spinning and weaving rather than to the state's ports for shipment as a raw material. Textile manufacturing continues as an important industry today, although tobacco is by far the state's biggest crop. North Carolina is, in fact, the largest tobacco producer in the nation

*Preceding page:* Charlotte's Mint Museum, a federal mint from 1835 to 1913, is now a treasure house of art that features a new exhibit on Spanish colonial artifacts. *This page, top to bottom:* Light floods an airy interior at the Public Library. Performance spaces, galleries, and classrooms fill Charlotte's Spirit Square. Fountains cascade in front of Discovery Place, a hands-on science and technology museum.

*Preceding page:* Spirit Square's 780-seat theater, a former Baptist church, incorporates the stained-glass windows of its previous identity. *This page, right:* Overcarsh House, a turn-of-the-century dwelling in Charlotte's historic Fourth Ward, offers bed-and-breakfast accommodations. *Below:* Graves date from 1771 in the Settlers Square Cemetery.

The dates that bracket North Carolina's initials on the state flag mark early resolutions to gain independence from Britain. *Below:* An equestrian statue of George Washington and a pair of Revolutionary cannons stand before the state capitol in Raleigh (1840).

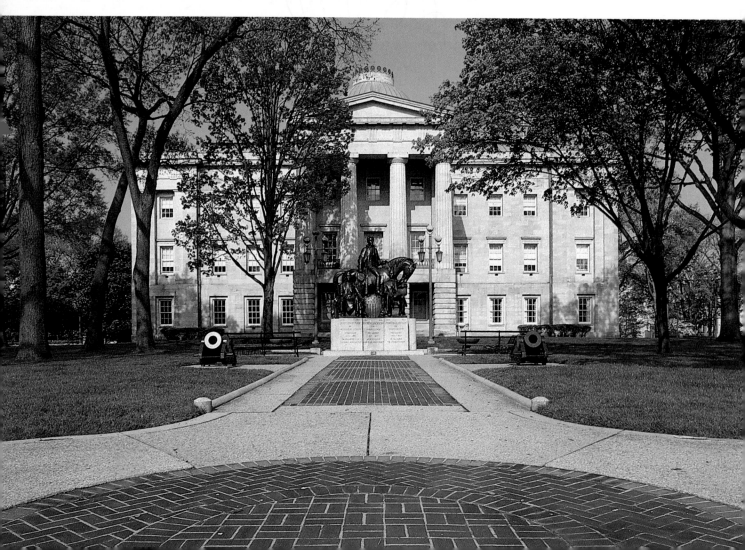

and the tobacco industry has contributed heavily to the state's educational and cultural institutions over the years.

While the English were the first Europeans to till North Carolina's soil, they were by no means the colony's only immigrants. Inexpensive farmland in the Piedmont, in particular, attracted newcomers from overseas to the mainland's river ports or south from earlier-developed mid-Atlantic areas where land prices were rising in the eighteenth and nineteenth centuries. Between 1732 and 1754, the colony's population more than doubled. Many of the new arrivals were either Highland Scots or Scots-Irish, farmers whose ancestors were originally from Scotland but who had lived for some centuries in the northern counties of Ireland. Each July, North Carolina tips its hat to its Scots heritage with a festival at Grandfather Mountain that attracts crowds upwards of 10,000. The Gathering of the Clans, the largest event of its kind in the eastern U.S., includes performances by bagpipers, Highland dancing, sheepdog trials, and the tossing of the caber (a telephone-pole-sized log) by large, burly Scots.

Groups of Germans, mostly from previous settlements in Pennsylvania, also swelled the ranks of North Carolinians in the late colonial days. In 1766 the Moravians, religious refugees

*Top to bottom:* Rippling water and blue sky frame the state legislative building (1963) in Raleigh. A Vietnam memorial stands before the state capitol portico. A marble George Washington wearing classical garb is encircled by busts of notable North Carolinians in the capitol rotunda.

This statue in Fayetteville honors Sir Walter Raleigh, the sixteenth-century adventurer who sponsored the earliest English settlement in what is now North Carolina. *Opposite:* Visitors to Raleigh may tour the Governor's Mansion, home of North Carolina's chief executives since 1891.

*Preceding page:* Fayetteville Street Mall runs from the capitol to the Civic and Convention Center in Raleigh. *This page:* A 116-foot granite bell tower (left) marks the campus of North Carolina State University. A broad plaza (right) sets off the university's D.H. Hill Library. *Below:* The City Market in Raleigh, built as a produce market in 1914, now houses antique shops and boutiques.

from what today is Czechoslovakia, established a community in Salem (now part of the city of Winston-Salem). Their industrious habits, sharing of social burdens, and refusal to take sides during the Revolutionary War made them both prosperous and respected. Nearly 100 restored buildings in Old Salem, a dozen of them open as museums, give visitors a taste of the cultured, communal life of the Moravian settlement. It's easy to imagine oneself back in nineteenth-century Salem as costumed guides interpret the exhibits and work at Moravian arts and crafts with the traditional tools.

Further east in the Piedmont is North Carolina's academic heartland. The University of North Carolina was the first state university in the country when it opened in 1795. UNC's dome-topped Old Well, once the source of water for the town and now a campus drinking fountain, is the center not only of the campus but also of Chapel Hill itself. This cosmopolitan town is the westernmost of three neighboring college communities. Nearby Raleigh, with its copper-domed State Capitol of 1840, is the home of North Carolina State University, and the towers of the Duke University chapel, modelled after Canterbury Cathedral, rise above Durham.

*Preceding page:* Mordecai House, a plantation dwelling built in 1785, has been preserved as a Raleigh historic site. *Below:* Now a museum of Victorian interiors, the house belonged to the Mordecai family until the 1960's. *This page, above:* Andrew Johnson, president of the U.S. from 1865 to 1869, was born in this 12-by-18-foot house, which now stands in Raleigh's Mordecai Historic Park. *Right:* This plaque explains that the Johnson house was moved from its original location on Fayetteville Street.

BIRTHPLACE OF ANDREW JOHNSON

ANDREW JOHNSON, 17TH PRESIDENT OF THE UNITED STATES, WAS BORN IN THIS HOUSE ON DECEMBER 29, 1808. AT THAT TIME THE HOUSE STOOD ON FAYETTEVILLE STREET.

IN JULY 1904, IT WAS PURCHASED BY THE COLONIAL DAMES AND LATER PRESENTED TO THE CITY OF RALEIGH.

*Preceding page:* At the National Humanities Center in Research Triangle Park, scholars from around the country further their research. *This page:* Government, industry, and academe collaboratively pursue knowledge at Research Triangle Park, set amid the pines near Raleigh.

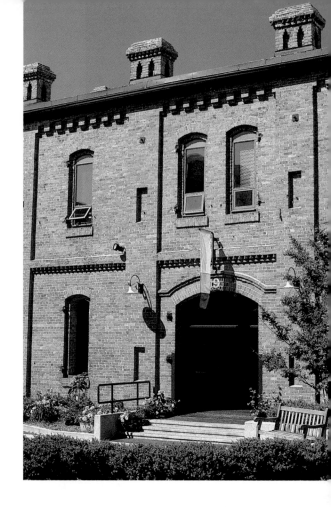

*Above:* Before the 210-foot bell tower (left) of Duke University Chapel in Durham stands a statue of the institution's benefactor, tobacco baron James B. Duke. The shops of Durham's Brightleaf Square (right) fill a onetime tobacco warehouse. *Below:* A Neo-Gothic quad adds a grace note to the picturesque campus of Duke University.

Industrial and civic leaders of the 1960's took note of this concentration of intellectual activity and sited in its midst the center of research and post-industrial progress known as Research Triangle Park. Today RTP's eight square miles make up the largest planned research park in the nation, with gleamingly modern facilities of academic, corporate, and government technology clustered in the shelter of tall pines.

Many Piedmont traditions are in flux. The region is increasingly industrial and commercial, both around Research Triangle Park and in the Charlotte area. The largest city in the Carolinas, Charlotte has a population over 350,000 and is still growing. Although corporate headquarters buildings, large industrial parks, and the international hub airport of the "Queen City" jar some of the old-timers in a state that is still mostly small towns and stretches of farmland, Charlotte's economic boom has brought benefits to the entire surrounding area.

Industry and commerce were less important in the Piedmont of 125 years ago when national conflict rocked North Carolina's country ways—and, in fact, changed the face of ordinary lives throughout the country. The Piedmont's small farmers were not, by and large, slave-holders, but they were the

*Top to bottom:* Nicknamed "Silent Sam" by the students of the University of North Carolina in Chapel Hill, this statue pays tribute to the 321 alumni of U.N.C. who died while fighting the Civil War. Old Well, U.N.C.'s traditional center, fronts the university's original building, Old East. The Intimate bookstore in Chapel Hill serves the literary needs of faculty, students, and townspeople.

*Preceding page:* A Winston-Salem skyscraper seems to spring straight up from a bright bed of azaleas. *This page, above:* A guide in period costume (left) sits before a restored shop in Old Salem, an eighteenth-century Moravian settlement in the heart of today's Winston-Salem. The Single Brothers' Workshop (right) once housed men from age 14 to the time they were married. *Below:* Gravestones form tidy rows in God's Acre, the Moravians' cemetery.

Leather buckets, the fire extinguishers of an earlier day, hang ready on wooden pegs.

The quiet dignity of this Old Salem kitchen evokes the peaceful culture of the Moravians.

primary source of the state's contributions, in the form of young male lives, to the war effort of the Confederacy. The state, which had a ninth of the Confederacy's population, furnished a fifth of all Confederate soldiers. 10,000 of the 40,000 Confederates killed in action were from North Carolina, even though the state was the last to officially join the war, seceding from the Union several months into the conflict in May, 1861. In part, this was because of the strong abolitionist traditions in the state, where the majority of free North Carolinians did not own any slaves. The largest Civil War battle fought on North Carolina soil took place at Bentonville Battleground, near Raleigh, within a month of the conflict's end in 1865.

West of the Piedmont rise the foothills of the Blue Ridge, the first of two great mountain ranges that slant from northeast to southwest across western North Carolina. Beyond them, the hazy outlines of the Great Smokies span the North Carolina-Tennessee border. Together, the ranges include more than 40 peaks above 6,000 feet. The Blue Ridge Parkway, a two-lane scenic highway maintained by the National Park Service, links Virginia's Shenandoah National Park with Great Smoky Mountains National Park. Designed to give motorists a variety of mountain views free of commercial

*Top to bottom:* Elegant private homes like this brick Georgian stand side by side with Old Salem's museums. Culinary herbs flourish in an Old Salem garden. Reynolda Village, built as a model farm on tobacco tycoon R.J. Reynolds' estate, is now a shopping complex.

*Above:* The Moravians' solid dwellings (left) wear their centuries gracefully. Stark simplicity is the hallmark of the Moravian Church (right) in Bethabara Park, the site of a Moravian settlement predating Old Salem. *Below:* Palisades like those that once encircled Bethabara jut upward behind an original millstone unearthed at the site.

Guilford Courthouse Military Park was created at the site of an important Revolutionary War battle. *Below:* Once the home of former North Carolina governor John Morehead, Greensboro's Blandwood was remodeled in 1844 to become the first example of the Italianate style in the U.S. *Opposite:* Tobacco the premier crop of this agricultural state.

*eding page:* A tiled octagonal tower gives the nine-story City-County Building (1927) in Asheville a flamboyant Art-Deco crown. *This* *e:* By contrast, the courthouse (above) is solid and sober in its classical details. The city's skyline (below) rises before a Blue Ridge backdrop.

The boyhood home of Thomas Wolfe, this Asheville house is the setting of his autobiographical novel, *Look Homeward, Angel. Below:* The interior recalls the 1920's, when young Thomas's mother took in boarders. *Opposite:* Near Asheville, millionaire George Vanderbilt lived in a grand manner at Biltmore House (1895).

intrusions, the 490-mile parkway includes 250 miles in North Carolina. As its name suggests, the roadway often runs along the top of the ridge, with panoramas of the forested countryside and distant towns spread out below, and sometimes passes through areas bounded by split-rail fences where self-sufficient upland farmers tended their livestock and grew their crops among the hills and hollows well into this century. Temptations lure parkway travelers from their cars— idyllic picnic and fishing spots, short loop trails to even finer views, centers that interpret the region's geology and natural history and showcase regional handcrafts. Not far off the parkway is Mt. Mitchell State Park, dominated by the east's highest peak.

In the midst of the mountain country lies Asheville. A refuge for those who longed to escape their steamy coastal homes in summer in the days before air conditioning, the Asheville area was a resort as far back as the Civil War. It surged in popularity around the turn of this century when wealthy New Yorkers discovered the charms of the cool foothills with their splendid mountain scenery. The grandest of the hotels built to accommodate this new group of summer people is the 1913 Grove Park Inn, with walls formed of local granite boulders and fireplaces that can hold 10-foot logs. The less well-to-do stayed in boarding houses, such as the one described in *Look Homeward, Angel,* Asheville-born novelist Thomas Wolfe's most famous work. The kitchen tables in his mother's 28-room boardinghouse, which is now a memorial to the well-known writer and his deeply autobiographical fiction, are always set as if in preparation for the boarders' supper.

*Preceding page:* Limestone appears lacy in the delicate carving (above) that trims windows and balustrades at Biltmore House, a 250-room mansion in the style of a French Renaissance chateau. The gardens and parkland (below) that surround Biltmore House were designed by Frederick Law Olmstead, the landscape architect of New York City's Central Park. *This page, top to bottom:* Walnut paneling and a marble fireplace enrich the two-level library. Luxury extends to this Biltmore bedroom, with its brocaded bed hangings. Wedgewood panels adorn a dining room fireplace, and tall gas lamps stand ready to illuminate the table.

*Preceding page:* A fountain with sculptures is the centerpiece of the glass-roofed garden room at Biltmore House. *This page:* The view from Cherry Cove Overlook (left) on the Blue Ridge Parkway takes in the granite mass of Looking Glass Rock. At the rustic stone Folk Art Center (below), east of Asheville on the parkway, the members of the Southern Highland Handicraft Guild display and sell their work.

Grandfather Mountain in the Blue Ridge rises to 5,964 feet. *Below:* The Appalachian Trail, a continuous footpath that runs from Maine to Georgia, traverses nearly 300 North Carolina mountain miles.

Asheville, long a center of the tobacco trade, is bordered on several sides by the Pisgah National Forest. Set in this idyllic landscape is Biltmore House, created by George W. Vanderbilt, the New York investor and heir to a fortune. Biltmore is the most popular traveler's destination in the state and the largest private house in the country. Vanderbilt bought a forest property of 125,000 acres and had his 250-room mountain house built there in 1895. French châteaux inspired Richard Morris Hunt's design, although the house had comforts unknown in medieval France—or, indeed, in much of the U.S. at the time—such as an indoor pool and a bowling alley. Frederick Law Olmstead, architect of New York City's Central Park, designed the surrounding terraces and gardens. The 75-foot-high front hall with its spiral staircase and ornate European antiques give visitors some sense of the life the heir of a railroad baron could lead in the days before income tax was invented. A trip downstairs adds a contrasting insight into the life of the 80-plus servants required to maintain the property in its heyday. When that day was over, the federal government acquired most of the surrounding estate; today it is part of the Pisgah National Forest.

*Top to bottom:* Many native Americans of the Cherokee nation, such as this dancer, now live on the Qualla Reservation, which borders Great Smoky Mountains National Park. Shops that offer products with native American motifs predominate in the town of Cherokee. In the Oconaluftee Cherokee Village, a craftsman follows the traditional methods of hollowing out a tree to make a canoe.

Hides hang on the wall of a cabin in the Oconaluftee Cherokee Village, which recreates the local life of two centuries ago. *Opposite:* Mingus Mill and the nearby Pioneer Farmstead give visitors to Great Smoky Mountains National Park a glimpse of a typical mountain farm that dates from about 1900.

Strong drafts that sometimes carry objects upward gave Blowing Rock in the Blue Ridge Mountains its name. *Below:* From Blowing Rock the land drops sharply into the Johns River Gorge.

*Above:* Flat Top Manor (left), the home of textile manufacturer Moses H. Cone, stands on the heights along the Blue Ridge Parkway. Cone's estate (right) encompassed 3,600 forested acres on and near 4,000-foot Flat Top Mountain. *Below:* The turn-of-the-century house is now a shop that sells local handicrafts. *Following pages:* Mountains, clouds, and light play a sunrise symphony along the Blue Ridge.

At the parkway's end lie the Smokies. Great Smoky Mountains National Park is within a day or two's drive of many of the most populated areas of the east coast. This fact, combined with its rugged and varied scenic splendor, makes it one of the most heavily visited of the country's national parks. Visitors can hike the extensive trail network, watch the wildlife and the tumble of mountain waterfalls, and look across the nearly endless succession of ridges, fading out to paler and paler blue at the misty horizon.

In many cases, they also travel to the town of Cherokee to watch the state's most-attended outdoor drama, *Unto These Hills*, the story of the tragic days when the Cherokee were pushed out of these mountains. For hundreds of years the Smokies rose over the country of an Iroquois group called "Mountaineers" by other native Americans. After many decades of war against the English and later, the American settlers, and more than a score of separate treaties, the mass of the Cherokee nation was expelled from the Appalachians and exiled to poor lands in today's Oklahoma. More than a third died on the forced march known as the "Trail of Tears." A small band fled into the mountains and remained fugitives for 30 years before they won the right to remain on their ancestral land. Descendents of this determined band, the Eastern Cherokee, make up most of the group of 8,000 native Americans who live today on the Qualla Reservation west of Asheville, the largest reservation in the eastern U.S. For them, as for many native and adopted North Carolinians over the years, North Carolina is the only place to be.

# Index of Photography

TIB indicates The Image Bank

| Page Number | Photographer | Page Number | Photographer |
|---|---|---|---|
| Title Page | Larry Ulrich | 37 | Nick Nicholson/TIB |
| 3 | Jonathan Wallen | 38 Top Left | Jonathan Wallen |
| 4 Top | Jonathan Wallen | 38 Top Right | Patti McConville/TIB |
| 4 Bottom | John Lewis Stage/TIB | 38 Bottom | Patti McConville/TIB |
| 5 (3) | Jonathan Wallen | 39 Top | Joe Devenney/TIB |
| 6 (2) | Paul Trummer/TIB | 39 Center | Juliana Ciminelli |
| 7 | Angelo Lomeo/TIB | 39 Bottom | Wallace Karault |
| 8 (2) | Nick Nicholson/TIB | 40 | Joe Devenney/TIB |
| 9 Top | Nick Nicholson/TIB | 41 Top (2) | Jonathan Wallen |
| 9 Bottom | Walter Gresham/ Roanoke Island Historical Association | 41 Bottom | M. Timothy O'Keefe/ Southern Stock Photos |
| 10-11 (2) | Nick Nicholson/TIB | 42 | Jonathan Wallen |
| 12 Top | Edward Slater/ Southern Stock Photos | 43 | Jonathan Wallen |
| | | 44 Top | Charles Brooks |
| 12 Bottom | Southern Stock Photos | 44 Center | Edward Bower/TIB |
| 13 | Edward Bower/TIB | 44 Bottom | Joe Devenney/TIB |
| 14 | Bullaty/Lomeo /TIB | 45 Top Left | Charles Brooks |
| 15 | Jack Ward/TIB | 45 Top Right | Jonathan Wallen |
| 16 (3) | Jonathan Wallen | 45 Bottom | Jonathan Wallen |
| 17 (2) | Jonathan Wallen | 46 (2) | Jonathan Wallen |
| 18 | Co Rentmeester/TIB | 47 | Sonja Bullaty/TIB |
| 19 Top | Chuck Lawliss/TIB | 48 | Charles Brooks |
| 19 Bottom | Jim Moriarty | 49 (2) | Charles Brooks |
| 20 (2) | Jonathan Wallen | 50 Top | Ned Haines/ Photo Researchers, Inc. |
| 21 | Charles Brooks | 50 Bottom | Mark E. Gibson |
| 22 | Nick Nicholson/TIB | 51 | Jagdish Chavda/ Southern Stock Photos |
| 23 (2) | Charles Brooks | | |
| 24 | Jonathan Wallen | 52 Top | Nick Nicholson/TIB |
| 25 (3) | Charles Brooks | 52 Bottom | John L. Nemeth/ Stockphotos, Inc. |
| 26 | Charles Brooks | | |
| 27 (2) | Charles Brooks | 53 (3) | Nick Nicholson/TIB |
| 28 Top | Nick Nicholson/TIB | 54 | Susan McCartney/ Photo Researchers, Inc. |
| 28 Bottom | Jonathan Wallen | | |
| 29 Top | Nick Nicholson/TIB | 55 (2) | Edward Bower/TIB |
| 29 Center | Patti McConville/TIB | 56 Top | Edward Bower/TIB |
| 29 Bottom | Joe Devenney/TIB | 56 Bottom | Bullaty/Lomeo /TIB |
| 30 | Nick Nicholson/TIB | 57 Top | Charles Brooks |
| 31 | Jonathan Wallen | 57 Center | Nancy Pierce |
| 32 | Patti McConville/TIB | 57 Bottom | Billy E. Barnes |
| 33 Top Left | Jonathan Wallen | 58 | Jonathan Wallen |
| 33 Top Right | Nick Nicholson/TIB | 59 | Larry Ulrich |
| 33 Bottom | Nick Nicholson/TIB | 60 Top | Nick Nicholson/TIB |
| 34 (2) | Jonathan Wallen | 60 Bottom | Jonathan Wallen |
| 35 (2) | Nick Nicholson/TIB | 61 (3) | Edward Bower/TIB |
| 36 | Edward Bower/TIB | 62-63 | Sonja Bullaty/TIB |